The Handbook of Quick Brand Building

By: Gage Glisson

Your brand will most likely fail. Most brands do, people get motivated and decide they want to be the next big thing in streetwear.

Those people forget to plan and think about the business aspect of starting a brand, so they fail. There are only a few successful brands out there and they did not get there by accident, they had all of the pieces to the puzzle. They planned, they designed, they marketed then set up sales channels, then they produced and lastly they marketed again

Starting a brand can be so fulfilling, there is just something about seeing people wearing and enjoying your designs. It can be hard though and starting a brand can take a lot of work. You just have to remember that people start brands for different reasons and each reason will have a different path to success. Some people start a brand to get famous, others do it just to make a few quick dollars. Then there is the type of person I am, I started a brand because it is my passion. I loved the idea of bringing together a community and creating content people can talk about and enjoy together.

.

Planning for your brand

The first step in any journey is the most important. Your brand could be anything that you want it to be, and with hard work,

dedication, and patients you can build a legacy.

The first steps to making your brand is just like

any other business. You need a brand story or

background, an expense sheet and your

marketing strategy

My brand is Leviathan Trading Co. I

make apparel for the people who love fast

imports, anime and pop culture. Our mission is

to make quality clothing for people who love

fast imports and anime. Simple. You get to your

mission statement after you think about the

backstory for your brand and narrow it down to something sellable and inclusive. The way that I found best to do this is to write down all the things you want to be associated with your brand, and it can be anything, any idea or any person. Make sure you have between twenty to 30 things, Any less than twenty and it will be too narrow and any more and it will be too inclusive. You want to hit a niche bigger than 10 people but you also do not want to try to sell to everyone. You would rather have one hundred people totally in love with your brand than one thousand people who think its cool but not cool enough to buy anything. What can help with this step the most is thinking about someone who is apart of the niche you are targeting. Think about the things they like, stuff they say, who their friends are and where they would hangout at. Those are the things you want to construct your list from.

After you have your list wait a week maybe even two, then go back and ask yourself why you chose that word to every single word on your list. This will help you really get an idea of what you want your brand to be about and then you can start to narrow it down to a single unified idea that you can turn into your mission statement. Knowing what your brand is about is a key part of the whole process, because once you know that you can decide what stores you want to carry your brand, what A or B influencers you want to be associated with and how to best market to your crowd.

The next step is to write down your business plan to help define your goals and achieve them. I know it sounds boring, but it is a very necessary evil to be successful. As much fun as starting a brand is you have to treat it like one if you want it to actually be profitable. Though the steps to it are simple, first you need to define the end goal of your brand. For me it was to create a cool and edgy clothing brand, next you need to define all of your goals and when you want to reach them. The milestones I wanted to reach were simple, one hundred website visits in the first month, 10 orders in the first 2 months and then to consistently grow those numbers by fifty percent for the preceding months. Next what you need to do is define how you are going to reach the goals that you set and write your ideas down. I went about this by doing gorilla marketing campaigns and social media marketing through B influencers. You also need to think about housing the goods, producing them and shipping costs. Remember that when you make a business plan you are not done yet the business plan will need to be revisited every season, because your products and goals will most likely change. The way you market one season might be completely different from the next as marketing strategies are constantly evolving.

Now remember that you do not want to rush any of this, take your time and make sure that everything is concrete. Your plan has to be something that you can stick to and that you are going to be able to scale and apply when your brand grows. The death of a lot of even successful brands happen when their brand grows beyond what their plan supports and they neglect to revise it to fit their new goals and needs.

The next big step in your business plan is to make your expense sheet. An expense sheet is an all inclusive list of the money that you expect to spend on your brand in the first few months. My expense sheet was simple I wrote down all of the cost of the blank goods that I wanted to print on and then I spent hours finding the best and most cost effective way to print on the goods. I also made sure to include a small ad budget so I could start marketing on social media right away.

It is key to write down the cost of everything you plan on putting money into. Find out how much it's going to cost for your prints and goods, marketing, website costs, shipping, packaging and anything else that you can think of that is going to cost you money. Make sure to ask the suppliers a lot of questions when doing this, the last thing you want is to run into unexpected charges like set up costs, run fees and upsize charges.

Go over your expense sheet a few times and make sure that you have on there everything that you plan on spending. After adding up all the costs it's going to look like a lot of money and then you want to raise that cost by twenty five percent to account for all the little extra stuff that is going to come up or be more expensive that you had originally thought. Starting a brand is not going to be cheap and if you are still wanting to start after seeing the price tag then kudos to you, because no one ever said it was going to be cheap, and if they did, they lied to you.

Now that you are ready to go with your business plan and expense sheet you need to take care of all of your legal paperwork to make your brand a legal business. First you need to decide on a business structure, such as an LLC, sole proprietorship or corporation just to name a few. Each one has their different benefits, drawbacks and processes to get started. If you do not plan on having any employees for a while start as a sole proprietor or partnership if there are two of you. Moving forward I am explaining the steps for a sole proprietorship because that is what I have done. When the business name is different from the owner's full legal name(s), the "Assumed Name Act" requires sole proprietorships and general partnerships to register the business name with their county clerk's office. This step can be done at your local county clerk's office. Then you need to get your federal tax id or EIN, this can be done for free on the IRS website.

The next step is getting your tax exemption most businesses are required to be registered and/or licensed If you plan to hire employees, buy or sell products wholesale or retail, or manufacture goods. The tax exemption form/resale license is required by most wholesale suppliers to be allowed to purchase from them so it is very important to have these forms. Be sure not to forget that your state will have plenty of resources to help you get all of the things you need to operate legally.

Initial design

Initial design is by far one of the best and most rewarding parts of starting your brand, it's the first step in bringing your ideas to life on a wearable medium. For me it didn't take long to get my first design ready because that idea is the reason I started the brand to begin with. I knew

that I wanted something that was going to draw

a lot of attention and had the brand name right in

the center of the artwork. The next two designs

came to me slowly but these things can take time

to think through, for example: take a look

around the internet at what the popular things to

put on apparel are and base your design off of

that. Make sure that you aren't copying,

originality is important. I had noticed that people

liked items that featured stuff related to manual

cars, so I thought about it for a while and came

to the idea for my button with a picture of a

manual gear shift that says endangered species on it.

Before you start into the next step of initial marketing you need to make sure that you have at least three solid designs that are going to show everything that your brand is about and nothing that it is not. You want to have a design that clearly has your logo or brand name in your first three designs. Having something with your logo clearly visible is important for brand building and making something to recognise you by. This design will also be the one that you want on your promotional items for giveaways or to wear around for marketing purposes. The other two designs can be fluff that your niche will really resonate with your niche, these designs will be a higher price and most likely not produced for an entry point item.

After you have decided on your designs you need to think about what clothing items these designs will best go on. The effect you want to have with your art will decide what color item or what type of item you want to attach it to. My main logo with my brand name most clear was white and red, I decided to put the image onto a black shirt as to draw more attention to the brand name because red stands out on both black and white and then the white would draw attention to the artwork as a whole. With a design you want to be more aesthetically pleasing you want to choose colors that compliment to your artwork so it is more pleasing to look at and blends well, this is better done with designs that have a lot of color and intricacy to them.

Initial marketing

Moving into the deciding step of this entire process, Initial marketing. Doing this step will tell you if you should pursue creating your brand or if you should go back to the drawing board. It is important to do this step before you buy a lot of product. By waiting to buy product you can mitigate a lot of the initial cost of starting a brand and help to ensure that you are not going to waste your time and hard earned money. At this stage if you are not able to generate a lot of interest around your brand you are easily able to back out and only have a minimal loss instead of putting all of your money into products then having to run around and search for customers who want the products.

The way to go about doing this is to produce a small entry point item or two that you can produce and then sell for a cheap price or give away in marketing promotions. The items I used were buttons and large decals, the idea is that I could have them made for a cheap enough price that I could give them away and not worry about the loss and sell some of them to make up for the few that I had given away. Another reason that I chose these two items is versatility. What I mean by that is that is that they could be put anywhere and out on display all the time when the customer goes out. Consider this, the button can go on a variety of things like bags, hats, seatbelts, shirts, jackets, and so many more things that people take with them everywhere. Its perfect cause the customer has something the can wear everywhere and you have tons of free marketing. You can't wear a shirt every day but you can have a button on you all the time. With the decal it is perfect for cars, laptops and binders. These are things people take everywhere and are constantly on display so I thought that making a decal was an obvious choice for me.

Though there are tons of other good items to consider like, magnets, lapel pins, lanyards and phone grips. The point of these items is to give away and show off on social media to see how much of a buzz you can get going for your brand without making any large products. If you wanted to take it to the next level once you have created buzz you can then start generating pre-orders for your products to take away more cost from your initial stock purchase.

A list of social media sites to market on:

- FACEBOOK

- INSTAGRAM

- TWITTER

- SNAPCHAT

- YOUTUBE

PRODUCTION

Now that you have gotten some people to like your brand enough to want to buy things you need to start producing your goods. This is why you made the expense sheet earlier, so you knew how much this would cost. Make sure that your supplier has good minimums and their cost is good for the production quality. Most suppliers have different specialties, you want to make sure that the supplier you choose is going to be good at what you are having made. Some are better at screen printing or direct to garment or even sublimation, and sometimes asi products. Just remember to play to the strengths of your supplier to make things easier for both you and them.

Another important thing to consider is stretch capability. Be sure to ask the supplier how large of orders that they can handle. If they are smaller but have a lot of orders it will be very hard for them to take on a large order with all of their other ones. Consider finding a supplier that will be able to scale with you business and have the flexibility for taking your small orders when just starting and huge orders as you grow. Sure you could find somewhere else if you outgrow the place that was making your goods, but relationship is important. Having a good relationship with your supplier is good because it can lead to: getting better prices, your orders being higher priority and more willingness to do favors. Relationships are built through dedicating a certain volume of business to a company or having used them for a long time.

Here is a list of good apparel decorating companies:

- Silkworm Ink

- Printful

- Custom Ink

Here is a list of good asi companies with a wide variety of products:

- HIT promotional products

- Leprechaun

- Uprinting

Once your products start coming in it is time to start setting up your inventory system and shipping area for best efficiency. What worked best for me might not work for you, it is important to find a system that will best fit your business and what you do. If you sell more in person or at events the way you set things up will be totally different than that of someone who sells completely online. I have kept all of my goods in boxes stacked in my storage room with the item and quantity written on the box that way I could just pull from the box and take it to my shipping area to sent it out. I also kept a small stock of goods in my trunk so I would always be ready to sell something or market to someone.

Everyone always wonders how best to price their products and it is pretty simple. It's also good to keep in mind that the higher quantity you order at a time from your supplier or manufacturer can lower your production cost so you can price more effectively for a higher profit margin. Also make sure that you include things like art, shipping costs and most importantly time into your cost. The best profit margin is around 50% to your average customer and 15%-20% to your distributors. For example: your total cost for a shirt is 9.85 for the shirt, decoration, shipping, art and set up you would want to multiply that by 1.50 to get your retail cost or "MSRP" which would be 14.77 for a 50% profit margin, and you could go higher if you wanted depending on average cost of apparel in your area and to sell to suppliers you want to give them a "net" cost normally 30%-50% lower than your retail cost that could be around 12.31 leaving them room to profit as well.

Shipping is another big factor in the cost of production and selling. Not only are you paying to get your goods to you but also to get them to your customer. There are so many different variables when it comes to shipping costs and everyone will have a different experience. Though in my experience for light things like most apparel USPS was the best option. USPS will send you free shipping supplies in a variety of sizes to fit what you need to ship. They have some of the best rates for shipping and can be great for just getting started. Also if you are in a hurry for supplies you can just pick them up at your local post office.

Though if you have to get things where they are

going very quickly fedex will be your best

option, they are the cheapest for overnight and

2nd day services at the time of writing this.

Making sales channels

With all of the pieces of the puzzle

coming together you need to be able to sell your

products. There are many sales channels

available and ideally you want to use all of them.

Though they all have the same effect they each

have a completely different process to set up.

The ones that are most commonly used are:

stores, websites and social media.

The idea of having your stuff in a stores everywhere is a common goal for a lot of brand owners. Stores are a great way to get sales and to circulate your products in your local area. Getting a store to carry your goods can be a pretty simple process but only if you are properly prepared.

There are a few things that you need to have before you ask a store to carry your brand, you need to have a good presentation of what your brand is and who you are, a product booklet, an order form,samples to show the purchaser. Let's say you find a local store that you want to carry your goods, what's the first thing you do? You want to call or go in and ask to speak with whoever purchases the products for the store and you would want to schedule a sit down with them, and remember to be as professional as possible. This process can seem a lot like a job interview and you should treat it as such, be on time, look presentable and have everything you need ready to go. After the introduction you should start off with showing them a presentation, introduce your brand and talk a bit about your mission and brand history.

Then you can go on to show them a product booklet with the prices they will pay (that would be around 20%-50% of the retail price as described in the production section) and the prices they can expect to sell your goods for(the price that you sell your goods to non wholesale customers at). Make sure that your product booklet includes all of your current products and a few that you plan on releasing in the future so they know what to expect. Lastly you can give them a few samples of your products to look at so they can see your quality of goods and some of the designs in person. Then you want to wrap up by giving them an order form or a number to contact to place their orders. The order form can be as simple as a print out spreadsheet with a place for quantity, item numbers and names. You could also have a website specifically for your wholesale customers.

The next most important channel of sale to have is your own website that people can connect with you and buy your products from. There are so many options out there for website building.

Just to name a few of the helpful sites for building your store:

- **SQUARE SPACE**

- **WEEBLY**

- **SHOPIFY**

- **WIX**

My favorite of those is shopify. Shopify makes it so easy to build you store and connect it to all of your social media outlets. With shopify it is also very simple to monitor traffic and build ad campaigns with the tools they have available. I highly recommend using them for your first online store, to add onto the long list of benefits they also sent you a card reader and a point of sale app for your mobile phone. To start you can make a thirty day free account on their website and use one of their easy to customize templates to build your website from. After you make your account you can start by selecting a template and customizing your front page. In my experience you want to have your brand name top and center and then use a section under it to describe your mission statement and who your brand is. Make sure to include links to all of your social media accounts on the front page so it is easily accessible.

Next you want to add your products to your store, shopify makes this very easy, all you have to do is add the item name, a picture and a description and you are ready to go. Be sure to include all variations of your product with the variation menus, also remember to spend some time writing in-depth and flavorful product descriptions for each of your items.

Your website should be close to finished, now you need to connect your store to your social media outlets like facebook, instagram and twitter. By connecting your shopify store to these sites you can easily build ad campaigns and manage posts on those from one place.

Your facebook and instagram page can also have options to sell products from them. Make sure to utilize these options when connecting your shopify page to these sites and it will set it up automatically. You can also take orders from your facebook messenger

There are so many sales channels available though they all have the same effect they each have a completely different process to set up and completely different audiences they reach, so it is important to make the best use you can of all of them.

FINAL MARKETING

Now that you have plenty of places to sell your products you just need a way to bring people to those places. If you did a good job with initial marketing you will already have people lined up to be on your site and in the stores you just need to tell them how to get there and lead the way. Another important thing is to keep growing your reach through influencers, social media and good old guerilla marketing.

Get your people in stores. If people go and buy your stuff in the stores that carry it they will be sure to order more. One of the best things you can do is ask the store owner to hold an event for the launch of your brand and give them some promotional items to give out. This will be sure to pull in your existing fans and make some more, doing this can also show the store how much reach and potential your brand has.

If you had a famous person to wear your brand you could almost skip all of the steps in this book. The truth is most people don't, not to worry because there are plenty of small influencers in most communities that would be willing to help you out just for some free merch. This can be so helpful for getting more people to participate in your brand. Lets say your brand was aimed at people who like art, then say you gave a bunch of merch to someone who has a large number of followers live streaming their painting sessions. People will be sure to ask where they got the stuff or even better they might talk about you on stream and say how nice you are for hooking them up, stuff like this can help to build a great image for you in your community. With a great image it is easier to engage with your community and seem less like someone who just wants to profit and more like someone trying to help bring people together and express their ideas and personality through the medium of fashion.

LEVERAGE. Leverage is the most important word when it comes to social media marketing, the more followers you have the more reach you have. You can also grow your reach and bring more people to your social media and website through well placed ads on places like: facebook, instagram, and snapchat. Instead of making posts all the time and blasting through all of your content quickly trying to spam posts you can leverage your money to make one post reach thousands of people more than a simple post could. By doing this you can bring so many more people to your website to show them all of your products and social media. Think of it as using a bucket to gather water instead of a spoon.

Another way you can leverage your influence is by asking other large pages to collaborate with you by exchanging promotions on each others page, this can also give you a lot of extra reach. When doing this, remember that you want their community to be closely related to yours so you're still hitting your target demographic and not wasting your time.

You now know plenty of places keep growing your reach through influencers, social media and good old guerilla marketing. If your business was a plant marketing would be miracle grow. Be sure to always be trying new and different marketing strategies, keeping your plan fresh is

the key to staying relevant in the constantly
evolving market.

THE FINAL STEP

You now have all of the pieces you need
to successfully build your brand. You know how
to plan, how to market, how to produce and how
to scale. The only thing standing in your way is
you. This book may not have answered all of
your questions but like all things the only way to
know everything is through experience. Though

now you know how to start, you have no excuses. Get going and be successful. Though remember it is going to be a long and hard road, do not give up, be patient, and keep trying. Not everyone is successful on their first try, if you fail to go back to the drawing board and think about where it went wrong. If you always learn from your mistakes one day you will be incapable of making them.

Good Luck

www.ingramcontent.com/pod-product-compliance
Lightning Source LLC
Chambersburg PA
CBHW061530250726

48657CB00005B/2165